Life in Verse

Sarabjeet Kaur

BookLeaf
Publishing

Presentation by *BookLeaf Publishing*

Web: www.bookleafpub.com

E-mail: info@bookleafpub.com

ISBN: 9789357216265

First edition 2023

MOTHER

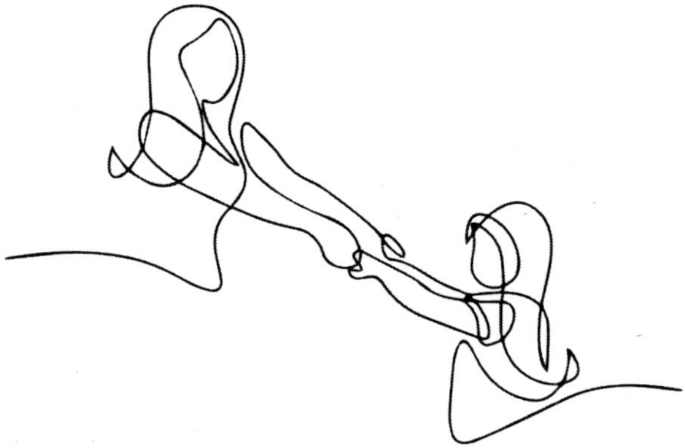

What a miracle is a mother!
A selfless being like no other

An epitome of love
A heavenly being from above

Lips adorning a beguiling smile
Eyes shining stars a mile

A harbinger of good tidings
Always daunting in her chidings

A confidante, friend and guide
Eyeing her children with pride

The pinnacle of strength and compassion
Full of vigour and passion

What a miracle is a mother!
A selfless being like no other

LITTLE GIRL

Once there was a little girl
With teeth as shiny as pearl

She was her parents' pride
And grew up to be a beautiful bride

Oh! What a sight to behold
With a cute smile and eyes rolled

Was mother's pet, father's princess
Loved by all I must confess

The memories are so precious
Lord above has been so gracious

My heart, my soul, my love
My angel descended from above

WINTER

A season of snow and sleet
A welcome respite from heat

Snow-capped mountains and hills
Braving oneself through winter chills

A season of revelry and fair
Looking out for everyone you care

The short days and long nights
Onset of magical yuletide

A season of family and friends
Each one dressing in latest trends

The warmth of the crackling wood
The snuggling blankets and long hoods

A season of affection and celebration
Of humanity and compassion

BELIEVE IN YOUR DREAMS

Believe in your dreams
Even if the head denies, the heart screams

People will always pull you down
Keep striving to achieve the crown

Fight the blocks in your way
It will come true one day

Don't deny yourself the pleasure
Of finding the beautiful treasure

There will be ups and downs
Takes a smile to dispel frowns

Don't let failure dampen your spirit
What the heart says, hear it

The universe gives ample signs
Follow them, trust in divine

Believe in your dreams
Even if the head denies, the heart screams

LIFE IS TOO SHORT

Life is too short for regrets
Don't stop to ponder and fret

Embrace what comes your way
Not letting determination sway

Triumph the doubts and sorrows
Live life as if no tomorrow

Value your friends and kin
So many hearts to conquer and win

People come and people go
What you reap is what you sow

Life is full of adventure
Everyday a diverse venture

Remembered are always good deeds
Beware the temptations, take heed

CHILDHOOD

Splendid memories galore
Full of numerous lores

Without a care in the world
Lying in mother's lap curled

The sweet innocence benign
Eyes as twinkling stars shine

Jumping in the muddy puddles
Wrecking the house in a muddle

Deprivation holds no meaning
A mischievous grin beaming

Shower of love and care
Protected by mother's prayer

Miss those days of fun and frolic
Time gone, makes heart melancholic

I wish I could rewind life
And escape this endless strife

I WISH

I wish there was no war
Turning life's memories sour

I wish no one was poor
Wealth in hands of fewer

I wish no one was sick
Happiness with a flick of magic

I wish there was plentiful
Prosperity, bliss in bountiful

I wish morals were high
Humanity, valour to swear by

I wish we all were one
No caste, no creed, no religion to shun

BUCKET LIST

Time seems to be rushing by
A speedy ageing one cannot deny

Ah! So long is the list
Let me apprise you in a gist

Want to travel the sphere
Places to me that are dear

Paris, London, Italy and Rome
A small world on its own

Paragliding is an adventure
The next thing on my venture

Exhilarating, speedy and nerve tingling
A sport worth experiencing

Aid the poor and deprived
Heartening to see lives revived

Before I leave this abode
Will walk the path which God showed

A DAY IN THE PARK

Fun and frolic of the kids
Chattering of the mothers amidst

Elderly walk quietly by
Park resounding with toddler's cry

A dog running to catch the ball
Joy to see the cute baby crawl

Ducks quacking away to glory
Children listening to grandma's story

Sitting under the tree with a book
The beautiful girl is given a look

A gentle breeze blows around
Carrying with it the wonderful sounds

A hush falls as the sun sets
Shadows become long against the silhouette

SCHOOL DAYS

As I reminisce the good old days
A warm and nostalgic phase

The sweet banter of friends
Following all the latest trends

Trips, camping and treks
Labs equipped with high-tech

Sports day, annual day and winter fair
Excitement abounds I declare

Recess time looked forward to
Chatting, playing, eating through

Learning the values of life
Preparing one for future strife

The precious moments are treasured
Giving us lifelong pleasure

WORST DAY OF MY LIFE

Shudder, as I remember the fateful day
Full of pain, sorrow and dismay

When mom was diagnosed with cancer
How serious it was no one had an answer

The time just stood still
With heavy heart, mustered the will

As days passed, physique was weak
Hopes of survival were bleak

Endured her pain with a smile
Seemed almost normal for a while

Painful to watch her day by day
Could do nothing but just pray

Her suffering made our hearts bleed
To remain calm and strong was the need

As she in my arms peacefully passed
End of torment for her at last

Will be in our memories forever
Ties with her will never sever

THE PANDEMIC

A pandemic! Everyone was shocked
Each one to one's home was locked

The streets, parks, roads so bare
The clear sky a sight so rare

Schools, offices, markets closed down
The air devoid of human sound

People in masks were everywhere
Follow protocols, no one was spared

Losing jobs and their earnings
Waking up to bleak mornings

Death, pain, sorrow surrounds
Hunger, strife, homelessness abound

True worth of human life realised
Precaution, prevention was advised

Wish never have to face it again
Give each strength and power to regain

HAPPINESS

Happiness is difficult to define
It's with sadness intertwined

The echo of the favourite song
Truly makes your will so strong

The twittering of the little bird
A lovable sound you've ever heard

Gentle breeze blowing through the hair
Calming the jittery nerves with care

Chirpiness of kids in the park
Melodious song of the lark

Glare of the sun so bright
Brings all my senses alive

Happiness is not hard to find
All whims and fancies of the mind

CHRISTMAS

Germanic pagan festival Christmas tide
To celebrate the birth of Christ

My favourite time of the year
Bringing with it the holiday cheer

Houses, places with adorned trees
Twinkling lights for eyes to please

Eagerly waiting for Santa to come
A Christmas tradition for everyone

Ginger-bread man, cookies and cake
Delicious turkey, casseroles and steaks

The hustle and bustle of the carnival
Celebrations galore of the joyous festival

Time to spread bliss and glee
To the deprived, unfortunate and needy

The year ends with positivity
Dispelling all doubts and negativity

TRAIN TO AMRITSAR

My childhood wish finally came true
Trip to Amritsar eventually fell through

Oh! I've waited so long for this
Seems to me, a heavenly bliss

Caught the early morning train
Began the journey, through lashing rain

Exhilaration filled my heart
As the train left the yard

The bogey resounded with voices
Reverberating with happy noises

The train ran past the green fields
Exhibiting proudly the ripe yields

Creating wonderful memories with family and friends
Wishing that time would not end

As we reached the destination
Mind, body and soul full of sensations

A memorable journey, hard to forget
With joyous moments, with no regrets

THE GOLDEN TEMPLE

A Sikh pilgrimage divine
A supreme presence benign

The reddish hue of the morning sky
The celestial aura mystifies

Melodious hymns drifting in the air
Teaching one to share and care

The holy water cures the ills
Surrounded by serenity and tranquil

The ambience so pure
Many devotees it allures

Defying status, creed or caste
An incredible history so vast

A memorable experience to behold
A journey worth being retold

DUBAI

A city of skyscrapers, ports and beaches
Tolerance to all religions it teaches

The hustle and bustle at the marina
Magnificent Burj Khalifa a prima

Amazing landscape of palm-shaped islands
Radiant amidst the sand like a diamond

Desert safari an exciting adventure
High on list of Dubai ventures

People so cordial and warm
Prime aspect of Dubai's charm

Enjoy the world’s tallest swing ride
Dubai parks are its pride

A place on my list of revisit
Diverse emotions the heart elicits

Abounding in memories galore
City to remember always, for sure

SINGAPORE

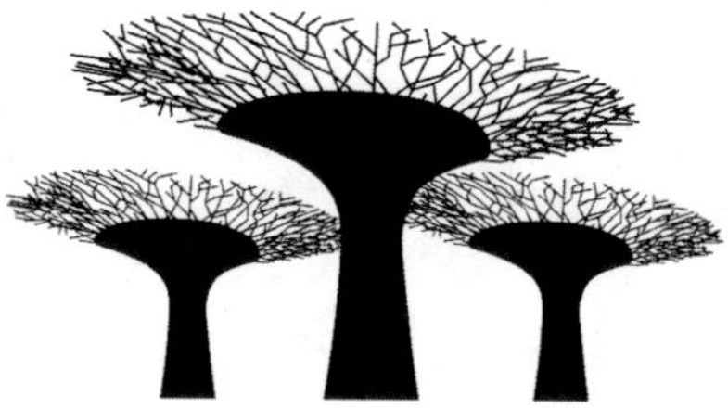

Boasting of lush green, eco-friendly malls
Skyscrapers that proudly stand tall

Night safari an experience unique
Sounds of animals to ear musique

Jurong bird park, a place of intrigue
Unmatchable site in its own league

Plethora of things to do in the city
Sentosa island Ah! So pretty

A perfect hub for travellers
Nightlife a treat for revellers

Diverse cuisine a treat to relish
Numerous experiences to cherish

The city is state of the art
Holds a distinctive place in my heart

MY FATHER

A pillar of strength and virtue
True to his promises life through

Fulfilling our demands with a smile
Not hesitating to walk the extra mile

Putting himself last and us foremost
Appreciated for being a wonderful host

Teaching diligently the ways of the world
Diverting each stone that was hurled

Crying in our sorrow, jubilant in success
Full of emotions, difficult to express

Praise the Lord who created him
Abounding in kindness, love but no whim

Gratitude, respect and affection
A symbol of complete perfection

Indebted we are for life to him
Charismatic aura that can never dim

DAUGHTERS

Those precious little things
Cherish and provide them wings

Will always stand by you
Through thick, thin and blue

Certainly a mother's best friend
A helping hand to lend and tend

Tears in their eyes break heart
Makes my mind so distraught

The adorable creations of God
Deserving a righteous applaud

Teach your sons to respect them
They are such precious gems

Don't kill them in the womb
You'll be answerable on the day of doom

BECOMING A POET

Was not on my bucket list
Let me explain in a gist

Inspired by my daughters to write
Believe their decision was right

The thoughts ran hither and thither
Took a while for them to gather

Was so unsure of the outcome
But built a steady momentum

Determining the topics was a task
Shortening the list, too much to ask

Followed the heart, fulfilled my passion
Dispelled the doubt and distractions

Finally the efforts bore fruit
To mom and dad, it's my tribute